Letters To Mothers

The Daughter's Edition

Letters To Mothers

The Daughter's Edition

By: Donnette Jones
Copyright © 2021 Donnette Jones

Letters to Mothers: The Daughter's Edition
Copyright © 2021 Donnette Jones
Published by Never A-Mis Enterprises, LLC
P.O. Box 2298
Byron, GA 31008-2298
www.neveramisenterprises.com

ISBN: 979895059700

Printed in the United States of America

All rights reserved.
No part of this publication may be reproduced, stored in a retrieval system, or transmitted in any form or by any means - for example, electronic, photocopy, recording - without the prior written permission of the publisher. The only exception is brief quotations in printed reviews. The authorized purchaser has been granted a nontransferable, nonexclusive, and noncommercial right to access and view this electronic publication, and purchaser agrees to do so only in accordance with the terms of use under which it was purchased or transmitted. Participation in or encouragement of piracy of copyrighted materials in violation of author's and publisher's right is strictly prohibited.

—DEDICATION—

I would like to dedicate this book to … my mother, Sandra Randle … a true praying woman. My oldest daughter Quisha, you are truly a gift from God. To my second oldest, Thank you for your true heart of love. My third daughter Stef; Thank you for challenging me on every turn it made me grow. Thank you to my fourth daughter; even thou we are in a difficult place at this moment you are still my sunshine! To my fifth daughter Ashlynn, you are an amazing person with gifts that are Golden. And to my sixth daughter Makayla, mamas baby girl; Truly God honored me when He gave me you, a true servant

Thank You!!

May The Pure Blessings of GOD rest upon ALL

of you!

~Apostle Donnette Jones~

Table of Contents

Introduction

Chapter One – "Blessings to a good Woman." Love, Donnette

Chapter Two – "I thank God you were my mama." Love, Sandra

Chapter Three – "A mother to me." Love, Jessica

Chapter Four – "I'm very grateful." Love, Keona

Chapter Five – "You are the definition of a mom." Love, Marquisha

Chapter Six – "The Ladder." Love, Stef

Table of Contents

Chapter Seven – "Dear mama." Love, Ashlynn

Chapter Eight – "Your Peter." Love, Trece

Chapter Nine – "Hey mom." Love, Trina

Chapter Ten – "Dear Mother." Love, Makayla

Chapter Eleven – "I love you momma." Love, Rochelle

About the Author

Introduction

I was entering my room and as I was about to sit on the bed, I heard the Lord say write a book from the heart of daughters to their mothers!

I jumped on the assignment not truly knowing what was about to unfold from my heart or the hearts of my own daughters (6). As my heart willed to obey, I begin to ask my own daughters to write and give me their feedback. What I received from each one was different. Some said, "Yes, mama" with a smile. One said, "No!" One was hesitant and the other thoughtfully was l like, "Uhhmmm I guess." I said, "Wait a minute, what is truly going on in the hearts of my girls?" Then it all began to unfold … Was it a possibility that you can laugh with your mama and talk to her every day, yet have hidden issues tucked deep away in a hidden compartment of the heart? Truly God had spoken. Each letter I read from my girls would be an eye-opener to me and other mothers. We could hear and see the heart of each daughter that wrote their TRUTHS!! I even have some to my mother!

Chapter One

"Blessings to a good woman."

Love, Donnette

Blessings to A good Woman. Mother, when I look back over the years of our mother and Daughter relationship, it is with great pleasure and with tears I can write this letter. I look back to see forward of how far we have come and overcome! You are Truly in my eyes a Good Woman! You always have been and always will be a Good Woman! No, not a perfect Woman ... you have made your mistakes and you have battled your demons to be free from all your pain & struggles. I see and know you won your fight against many things you were bound by and entangled with! You are Truly a Good Woman! I have seen your tears and heard your fears; but your inner beauty and fight was stronger; you stayed alive! Be all God created you to be! You came out; you came thru when the odds were not in your favor! You SURVIVED shame; abuse; abandonment; divorce; Lock ups and Lock Downs! You are a Good Woman! You forgave again and again and again, time after time after time! You are a Good Woman!

Your cry was heard from the Heavens. Your tears were seen like running water. Your moans and groans were felt by The Father. He made you Remarkable and Unbreakable! You are a Good Woman! Through sweat, blood, and tears you regained the years the canker worm and locust ate up! By God's Divine Grace you wouldn't give up and you strived to survive; you made it up; never look back! You are a Good Woman! The Joy I feel; the Peace I hear; and the Warrior I see now is why I live and become a Good Woman! I see a Perfect Picture when I look at you! YOU ARE A GOOD WOMAN!

Our Struggles were never in Vain, they were just a Reflection of His Amazing Grace.

You are a good woman! You are my girl!

I love you mama!

Chapter Two

"I thank God you were my mama."

Love, Sandra

Mama, I wanted to write to you and let you know that I love you and miss you very much. I didn't understand our mother daughter relationship. I always felt like you didn't love me, so I felt rejected. Now that you have left me, I began to think about our relationship. God opened my eyes to understand that you were being the best mother you knew how to be!

I thank God, He gave us an opportunity to spend time together before He took you home. I got to know you in a very special way. I was so grateful to God to be with you and take you through the sinner's prayer; I learned you knew Jesus. I know we all will see each other again. The Lord showed me a vision of us running in a field of green grass and flowers!

Love you mama. I thank God you were my mama!

Love always,

Your daughter, Sandra Randle

Pastor Sandra Randle

is the founder and pastor of "Rise up in His Glory Ministry" where they have come to set the captives free and heal the broken hearted. She is a caregiver. She has one daughter; eight grandchildren; and four great-grandchildren, who all love the Lord.

Chapter Three

"A mother to me."

Love, Jessica

Thank you for being a mother to me; staying on me, showing me what life and being a woman and mother was. I know it was hard with two kids on your own, yet you did it flawlessly. You were my best friend. Now that you are gone, who is going to love me like you? It's hard to love someone because I'm looking for your love from them. When I don't get your love, I push them away because that's what I desire. I need the Lord to help me stop seeking you in others and help me seek you in God. I need to heal from your death and make you even more proud of me. It's hard not having you call me or waking up to you in my house cooking, talking, or making noise. I miss us laying on our phones, not saying a word, chilling.

I really miss you. For a long time, I was mad at you for leaving me when you knew I needed you for everything. I saw you as my protector when it came to everything. You dealt with the bad so I could see the good in everything and everybody.

Chapter Four

"I'm very grateful."

Love, Keona

Dear Kimberly Moore,

Hi Mom, it's me, Keona as you can see. I'm very grateful that at 31 years old, I understand your role/position as a mother even though I don't have any children yet. I understand at this age, being a mother must have been hard. I understand the sacrifices each and every time we talk; working two jobs; coming home to make sure we ate; getting a little rest and waking up to punch a clock; again. I vaguely remember the times we had to be quiet while you were sleeping. I know working two jobs and taking care of three children had to take a toll on your body; only to do it with what looked like ease to me. Wow! I can imagine the many tears you cried. We only saw you burst from the room with your superwoman. Mommy you never showed a sign of weakness, you were always tough. Your version of training up a child in the way they should go was difficult for when it came to your disciplinarian actions and methods. Even though I didn't understand, you raised three kids to grow up and understand morals and values that kept us out of jail or dead.

      The "go-getter" mentality you've showed my entire life shows in my siblings and me! I know we all have made you very proud of the career paths we embarked upon. Thank you for loving us in your very own way. May God keep you in His will.

I love you Mommy!

Dear Donnette Jones,

Heyyyy Ma …My bonus mother! I remember I would ask you were we kin because of your former last name. I'm grateful God placed you in my life. It was bumpy in the beginning, but God kept us all! LOL! You were the one who taught me to be unapologetically me, Spiritually. You allowed me to pray, praise and meditate at a young age; more importantly be comfortable with the gift of speaking in tongues. I've grown to admire the way you allow the rest of my siblings and I tell you things freely. It's very important. I have witnessed you take on your "truths" and own them. Watching you taught me to own the skeletons in my closet as well; it may hurt but stand. Thank you for giving me Ashlynn and Makayla. God knew what He was doing all along. Keep your head up and God has the rest.

Thank you for learning to love me, your bonus daughter!

I love you Ma!

Chapter Five

"You are the definition of a mom."

Love, Marquisha

Dear Momma,

It has been an awesome journey being your daughter; even though sometimes was it was rough! LOL! Being a daughter of a woman who was still learning about herself was a crazy journey. I didn't realize you were still learning about you until I was older. As a child I looked at you as a superhero, a super mom. Growing up had to learn parents made mistakes and are human beings just like everyone on earth. You were a child raising children and that had to be stressful for you. A lot of things you didn't get to enjoy because you were being a mom; holding things together so they wouldn't fall through the cracks. You were our protector, our guide, and anything else we needed you to be for us. Honestly, you were a kickass mom! You made it look easy!! If we were suffering, we didn't know until we got older.

I appreciate you for the times you didn't give on your kids or do away with us. I thank you for not allowing the stress of being a young momma take over you and making a decision that would hurt us. Momma, writing this letter, reminds me of the fear you had when I was younger, and you didn't want me to be a fast girl. You put fear in my heart for a long time. At this point momma, you are truly forgiven because your preventative care for us was right; your methods were jacked up, but you did what you knew to do. I thank You Jesus that He kept you through all of this. You are an awesome mom. You got most of your kids to the age of 18 before they started wilding out! LOL! That's a BLESSING!

YOU TRULY ARE THE DEFINITION OF A MOM!

Chapter Six

"The Ladder."

Love, Stef

When most people think of a journey, they think of an open road with at least one vehicle; or they may think of a photo book full of memories. When I think of our love journey as mother and daughter, I think of a ladder. I think of how a ladder can be laid flat on the ground and used like a hopscotch game to jump into the open spaces. I think of how a ladder can be carried on a person's back by several people: or on a person's shoulder. I think of how we have carried each other through different times in our lives. You carried me when I was being formed in your womb. You jumped through the open spaces with me as you pushed me out and carried me through my youth.

Throughout my school years, you continued to jump through those spaces with me while you laughed, smiled, and shed tears. You taught me how to maneuver to the next step even when you had to hold my hand or lift me up a little.

As I got older; work got harder; and words from peers became meaner; you taught me how to carry my ladder to the field. The field had vividly beautiful trees; flowers of all colors and varieties, and all the good thing's life holds. You taught me how to place my ladder against the tallest tree in the field and to the top. First, you went ahead of me, once I learned how to climb it, you followed behind me. You taught me how to use the ladder to step out onto the branches of the tree. When I got scared or went a little to the left or right, you were there and pushed me back to safety. You taught me to see myself standing at the top of the tallest tree so I would be able to see all the other trees and the beautiful flowers. You pointed out the beautiful birds that were flying high and how to listen to their tunes so they could comfort me. At the top of the tree, you showed me which flowers were full of weeds and which ones had the snares. You taught me which trees produced good fruit, just in case I wanted to eat something other than what was on my tree. You taught me which trees I could visit if I wanted shade. You taught me which trees and flowers would take me to euphoric places could strangle or stunt my growth. You taught me the path back to my tree; you taught me to always use my ladder to climb my tree no matter how tall it got; I just had to extend my ladder.

Now, most of the trees in my field have left and went to their won field or are too distant and too far for me to walk. You have brought me plenty of other women with ladders of their own who were willing to sit in my tree with me. The women let me know it was okay to cry in my tree; it was okay string lights in my tree branches; and engrave art at the trunk of my tree. The women told me it was okay to dance around my tree when they brought music with them. The women used their voices to help me see the bright colors of the sky to replace the colors from some of the plants full of euphoria.

You carried me and my ladder on your shoulders in the earlier years of my path until I found a truck. The pick-up truck helps me carry my ladder so I wouldn't have to carry it so far or for so long. You taught me how to park my truck near a tree for shade when there weren't any trees to visit in my field. You taught me about all the other types of trucks in the world, other types of lights and other types of beauty. You taught me the best way to keep my lights from fading. You encouraged me to be balanced. You taught me how to plant my own flowers around my tree; how to weed my own plants; and how to create beauty in my own field. You encouraged me to see my own beautiful field as the best field amongst others. You pointed out the height of my tree and encouraged me to keep climbing even when I wanted to stay at the bottom in the shade. You encouraged me to climb my tree; to be safe and stand on its branches just as we'd done in my younger days. This time, you told me to shout of the beauty I saw in my tree for others to see near and far.

    You taught me life. I know as long as you're here, I can pull up in my pickup truck called life; with my ladder on the back, and you will teach how to carry, lift, load, climb, and maneuver my ladder to move ahead in my journey.

I pray I get to have more memories and more joyous climbs with you, always near my ladder.

You are loved, purely … by Stef.

Chapter Seven

"Dear Mama."

Love, Ashlynn

Dear Mama,

If I could choose one word to describe you, it would be "intense". You are one intense woman. It can be intimidating sometimes, but I absolutely admire it; especially when it comes to your work ethic and values. However, sometimes you can be a little too intense. One thing I have learned from you is the rake and shovel. I've learned how to rake in some your good qualities for myself, and shovel away the not so good stuff. No one is perfect. A person who always tries to be their best and learn from their mistakes is someone I admire, and I always want to be around.

      In my eighteen years of living, I have never left your side; and I don't plan to in the near future either! I thank God often for birthing me into our family and giving me a mother who has grown in God and continues to grow in Him. You keep me accountable, and I appreciate you for that. You have encouraged me on my journey of building my own relationship with Christ and coming to terms with myself. You have always been supportive of me and my dreams. Your honesty is brutal yet crucial to me. I don't know what I'd do without you, mama. You are the reason for my existence, and I wouldn't change you being my mother for anything in the world. After God, you are the most important person in my life. You have my respect, my love, and my trust. You make me want to be a better person and daughter of God.

    Thank you for genuinely being always yourself. Thank you for teaching me so much about this world and the people in it. I know when I really get into the world, I will be equipped with everything I need. I don't ever wanna forget the long talks and lectures you've given me and my siblings. I am not afraid to lose you because I know exactly where you're going. I am excited for you, and I know I will see you again. I will cherish your company while you are here and do my best to be as loving to you as you have always been to me.

Love,

Ashlynn

Chapter Eight

"Your Peter."

Love, Trece

Dear Mama,

I don't know how to start this letter. There are so many things I have wanted to talk to you about, I just didn't know how. For years I have been wondering why it seems to me that what happened to me years ago got swiped under the rug; it was never talked about again. It was never mentioned unless you are preaching or you're testifying about how God brought us through it. The night you found out; I was so ashamed. I felt like I brought shame on you and the family. I have felt for years you shaded me away. I have been thinking you was mad at me and the same situation was disgrace in your eyesight. From then on, I felt very distant from you. I felt like I had to hide myself in a box because I was afraid to share or show my feelings.

    For years I have felt nothing about me mattered. Years of feeling ashamed; years of feeling embarrassed of myself; years of not having a voice. Years of being disrespected, because I felt as if I wasn't given the respect of others and the ability to ever respect myself or anything of mine. I felt as if I wasn't welcome in your space, and if I was, only for a second. I guess I felt as if I was shut down and only allowed speak if it was necessary. I felt unnoticed and unwanted; that's why I would come and run at the first sight of trouble or an uproar.

    I also felt detached from you when I talked about the balloons you brought to school for my birthday. For years I have regretted that moment because you limited the things you did for me. I realize I hurt your feelings. I really apologize for it. I was really just having fun and being goofy, yet you took it to heart, mama. The incident that happened two years ago … Boy, I blamed everybody because again because I fell on my butt.

    I am so grateful for you. I love you mama. You are my queen. You have endured a lot and survived it. Many have counted you and your kids out; yet you kept pushing. You kept us motivated to keep going and not to let anything stop us. No woman on earth can compare to you. You are very strong, wise, beautiful, head strong, ten toes down for us, and very loving. God blessed me with the best mother possible. I love how our relationship is growing. I love you my wonder woman. God brought us through the darkest time. I am blessed to call you mama.

Your baby girl; tha 2nd.

Your Peter.

P.S. Stay free and keep being the fireball.

Chapter Nine

"Hey Mom."

Love, Trina

Hey mom, it's me; your youngest daughter.

Mom, as babies we grow; we learn and love. As parents, you teach, you love … and repeat. Growing up as your seed caused me a lot of grief and confusion. I was taught to lie, steal and cheat. I was taught to do whatever it takes to please your man. I was taught to cater to him as if he is the only KING; and quietly get beat. I was taught to use whatever necessary to keep him; even if it's pushing your kids to call him "daddy" even if he is not the father.

Momma, I grew up loving you no matter the flaws. I didn't care how you used or abused me emotionally. I could never understand why you never told us you loved us. Why no hugs and kisses … but as kids, we only think about what we need.

Before I move forward, I want to be the first to apologize to you for all those who dropped the ball with you. It wasn't you're doing, but it became your problem.

As I watched my friends' parents push them to greatness, I often wondered why you didn't push us. Why weren't you so involved like other parents? As I grew up, I found out a lot about you grew up. Things I wish I knew sooner, rather than this late. How did you not receive the love and nurturing you needed? How could I demand it when it was never demonstrated to you properly? Or how you got pregnant early, and your dad made every step of the way hard for you? He punished you for a mistake that severely changed your life. Thank you for being there for me and helping me when I made the same mistake. I remember you putting me and my sister in a stroller and walking from the dead end of MLK and Belfort to work at JITB to make ends meet for us.

  I apologize I didn't see your love. I didn't realize it was in the providing for us. You made sure we had food on the table and clothes on our backs. As a single parent working to make ends meet meant you not always being there for us to have roof over head. You taught us things you thought we needed to survive. You said when we learned better, we did better; whether we were receptive or not is a different story.

I now realize you gave us your ALL! You pushed me on a man because you wanted someone to love. I apologize your father didn't demonstrate love properly to you. Love is so powerful, it's like water to a flower.

Momma, please forgive me, I was a child and couldn't see. I couldn't see the sacrifices you made and the exchanges you made. I thank you a million times over for loving me your way, and for everything you gave up for me and my sister; for every end you made meet to take care of us.

Most importantly, I am elated you gave your life to Christ!

Love, Trina

Chapter Ten

"Dear Mother."

Love, Makayla

Dear Mother,

I only give you the words from my heart ... I've seen many come and many go. As it is past and present, one thing has remained growing in strength: my love for you and yours for me. It's true, I've come to know no other love as yours. You bring me joy none other can bring. You are the one who has wiped my tears away and nurtured me. In every way you care for me brings me peace. You truly are the only who understands me in times I've failed to understand on my own. I doubt anyone will know me as you know me. When I can't put words to how I feel, are there.

    You have laughed with me, and you have cried with me. I appreciate you so much because during my hard times, you've been there through every moment. All of those times make no difference to a woman like you; you love me the same. You make times easy.

    You have shown and taught me how to be grateful. You've shown me how to withstand hate from the greatest places and go to the lowest places where it may be. You've seen me at my lowest; helped me in my faults yet loved me the same.

After all of this is said and done, I am convinced you are the one I can come talk to; reminisce with; or just to be there for a warm hug and kiss! You are **MORE** than understanding … **MORE** than phenomenal!

Thank you is what I have to tell you!

Love, Your Sunshine – Makayla

Chapter Eleven

"I love you momma."

Love, Rochelle

Dear Momma,

I love you ♥♥♥

Love, Your Difficult & Direct Child – Rochelle

About the Author

APOSTLE DONNETTE JONES

Apostle Donnette Sherri Jones is the founder and Apostle of Divine Servitude Reaching Ministries. It is a ministry that is effectively changing lives by reaching people where they are and pulling them to where they should be.

Apostle Jones has a Prophetic mantle that is very accurate. Signs and wonders follow the Prophetic words she has released. She releases prophetic words of Fire; warning; healing; restoration; and life.

Apostle Donnette truly has a heart to minister to God's people and does so as opportunities present themselves; no matter the setting (church; grocery store; or parking lot). She reaches people by crossing over religious and racial barriers. You don't have to be a particular person or live a particular lifestyle for God's Word to minister to you when you are in Apostle Donnette's presence.

As an author and conference host, Apostle Jones hosts conferences in Houston; and other cities in Texas (Center, Lufkin, and San Augustine). She also travels to other states and cities to host conferences. Apostle Jones launched an Apostolic Empowerment Conference "Enforcing the Real" in 2016; a Prayer summons in 2016; and "The Prophets' Panel" in 2015.

She has ministered on conference calls, radio talk shows, and blog talk radio. She is the author of "Women 2 Women: Real Life Anecdotes". She has co-authored a collaboration with other apostles called "21st Century Women Apostles".

Apostle Donnette is a wife; a mother of eight and a grandmother of four.

BOOKING INFO

dsrmglobal@gmail.com

Facebook = Divine Servitude Reaching Ministries

www.ingramcontent.com/pod-product-compliance
Lightning Source LLC
LaVergne TN
LVHW051151080426
835508LV00021B/2585